Contents

INTRODUCTION

SIBO

Small Intestinal Bacterial Overgrowth (SIBO) is a digestive disorder characterized by excessive bacteria in the small intestine.

These bacteria then ferment (interact with food particles and nutrients) to cause a wide range of symptoms. Unlike the large intestine (also known as the gut or colon), which contains most of your gut bacteria, the small intestine should not have a large amount of bacteria.

SIBO is uncommon in young and middle-aged adults, but is thought to occur in at least 14% of older patients on average.

small intestine and large intestine SIBO

the elemental diet is a great way for patients struggling with GI issues, nutrient absorption or a wide variety of other health issues to absorb important nutrients through their diet!

The benefits associated with both full elemental and semi-elemental diets are well documented. While there are some formulations such as Vivonex Plus, which are hard to tolerate, there are a couple other products available, such as Absorb Plus, that can help make this diet a little easier on your taste buds.

With over an 85% success rate, particularly in patients with SIBO, the elemental diet is a clearly valid and highly recommended treatment option that may help you.

SIBO

What Is SIBO?

Small Intestinal Bacterial Overgrowth occurs when the small intestine becomes overrun with bacteria that don't belong there. Humans are hosts to trillions of microbes (bacteria, yeasts and viruses) that live on and inside of our bodies, especially our digestive tract.

When all is going well, we enjoy a symbiotic relationship with most of them, especially the helpful types that reside in our colon. You might know these helpful types as probiotics — the good bacteria and yeasts living in our gut that help build up our immune system, digest dietary fiber and keep our health in good working order. In the case of SIBO, problems arise when bacteria (even the good kind) begin colonizing in high numbers where they don't belong — in the small intestine.

The small intestine is the longest section of the our digestive system, spanning about 20 feet long, and is responsible for the absorption of certain nutrients, especially vitamin B12 and fats . When bacteria are present in higher-than-normal numbers in the small intestine, they interfere with absorption, causing nutrient deficiencies and gastrointestinal distress (gas, bloating, cramping). The bacterial overgrowth can also generate inflammation, causing damage to the gut's mucosal lining and inducing leaky gut syndrome.

Diagnosing SIBO and Recognizing Symptoms

Because SIBO symptoms overlap widely with other digestive issues, such as IBS, Crohn's disease and celiac disease, diagnosing SIBO can be challenging. The most common method for diagnosis is a lactulose breath test. Patients follow a specific diet for 12 hours and then fast for the following 12 hours. They then consume the lactulose solution and breathe into the testing device at various points for the subsequent few hours.

These tests, while not considered 100 percent reliable, use breath analysis to ascertain whether hydrogen or methane-producing bacteria are present in the small intestine. An overabundance of methane gas is associated with constipation, while an overabundance of hydrogen is associated with diarrhea. Because these two symptoms directly contradict or can happen intermittently if both gases are abundant (as is often the case with IBS), initial misdiagnosis is common. The results of a breath test can sometimes be the only difference between a SIBO diagnosis and an IBS diagnosis.

Typical SIBO symptoms include:

Diarrhea

Constipation

Gas

Bloating

Abdominal cramping

While in more severe cases, symptoms can elevate to:

Dramatic weight loss (due to malabsorption)

Steatorrhoea (fatty stool due to malabsorption)

Malnutrition

Vitamin B12 deficiency (due to malabsorption)

Liver lesions

Skin disorders (like rosacea, eczema, acne or rashes)

Leaky gut syndrome

Anemia

Oedema of lower extremities

These more severe symptoms are often comorbid with other diseases that can either exacerbate SIBO or be exacerbated by it. Additional symptoms include nerve pain (due to a B12 deficiency caused by SIBO), joint pain, depression, asthma, fatigue, nausea and vomiting.

What Causes SIBO?

The human body has a number of built-in mechanisms to keep our microbial guests in check, both in number and in location. We have gastric juices in the stomach that kill most living microbes before they reach the small intestine.

Intestinal motility and the migrating motor complex (MMC) both prevent putrefaction inside the intestine. Motility is the movement of the food bolus through the digestive tract, while the MMC sweeps the intestines between meals to collect any residual particles that could be hiding. The ileocecal valve separates the small and large intestine, acting as the gateway between the two sections of the bowel and locking off the billions of flora in the colon. Finally, we have bile secretions from the pancreas that kill off anything that's made it past the stomach acids. Disruption or weakening of any one of these protective mechanisms can open us up to bacterial overgrowth and cause SIBO.

Stress

A little-known fact: Stress can profoundly affect the protective mechanisms we've just laid out and is one of the underlying causes to a number of digestive disorders. You may have noticed your own digestion change during a stressful time in your life if you've experienced butterflies in your stomach, indigestion or intestinal cramping.

A 2005 study on mice indicated that psychological stress significantly slowed small intestinal motility, increased the presence of the E. coli bacteria, and damaged the mucosal lining of the small intestine. In healthy hosts, the bacteria inside the digestive tract work to keep each other in a state of equilibrium, but this study showed that the protective features of Lactobacillus bacteria diminished, allowing E. coli to over-colonize and disrupt regular gut function.

In addition to altering motility and colonic transit, certain types of stress have also shown repeatedly to alter visceral sensitivity, which might explain those cramps and bowel pain during stressful situations.

Stomach acid production is greatly heightened in highly stressful situations as well, which might suppress mucosal immunity and allow damaging bacteria like H. pylori (the bacteria implicated In gastric ulcers) to proliferate. The problem compounds itself when a chronically stressed individual opts to use medication to alleviate heartburn rather than addressing the underlying cause of the stress in their life.

Long-term use of proton-pump inhibitors like Prilosec or antacids like Pepcid AC or Zantac can also allow SIBO to take hold. They reduce the production of stomach acid, sometimes to a low enough level that would allow live bacteria to pass from the stomach into the small intestine.

Other Factors

Beyond stress, other underlying causes of SIBO include "anatomical abnormalities: small intestinal obstruction, diverticula, fistulae, surgical blind loop, previous ileo-cecal resections, and/or motility disorders (e.g. scleroderma, autonomic neuropathy in diabetes mellitus, post-radiation enteropathy, small intestinal pseudo-obstruction)," along with a number of diseases and syndromes.

Many of these diseases involve a vicious circle where SIBO exacerbates them while they also exacerbate SIBO. These diseases include Crohn's, celiac, diabetes mellitus, certain diseases of the liver and immunodeficiency syndromes like AIDS.

Curing SIBO

SIBO is a complex syndrome and requires multiple interventions to cure it. It's often a chronic problem, requiring cyclical treatment and regular intervals of testing and retesting in the event of persistent symptoms.

Dietary interventions that reduce inflammation and starve the misplaced bacteria have proven effective at reducing the uncomfortable and potentially damaging effects of SIBO, but they can't fully eradicate the harmful bacteria on their own.

Prescription antibiotic treatments or herbal antibiotics administered by a naturopathic doctor are necessary for comprehensive SIBO treatment. These treatments target the types of bacteria colonizing the small intestine.

Ongoing stress-reduction practices and lifestyle changes will help prevent recurrence and are critical to effectively treat SIBO. It's important to work with a doctor familiar with a holistic protocol for treating SIBO, as general antibiotics — especially if repeat treatments are necessary — are not recommended, nor is the use of antibiotics a complete solution to the problem. Tackling only one area of the three-fold approach of diet, medication and lifestyle change won't be enough to properly treat SIBO.

The SIBO Diet

To treat SIBO with dietary changes, your first goals are to manage the symptoms and stop the damage. Your next goal is to nourish the gut and encourage it to heal and rebuild itself with specific foods.

Many holistic medical professionals will recommend starting off with the strictest version of the SIBO diet — one that combines aspects of the SCD diet (Specific Carbohydrate Diet) and GAPS diet (Gut and Psychology Syndrome), but also restricts further by only allowing very low-FODMAP foods. Quite a few acronyms! Don't worry, we'll explain.

The goal in both SCD and GAPS is to promote healing of a damaged digestive tract through nutrient-dense foods that are easy to digest. Patients with IBS, IBD (inflammatory bowel disease), Ulcerative Colitis or Crohn's disease might try one of these diets to help alleviate their conditions.

GAPS, which is a more detailed and nuanced protocol, actually grew out of SCD research. It incorporates gut-healing foods such as bone broth and fermented juices and vegetables with every meal.

While these two protocols promote healing in a damaged gut, treating SIBO requires more restrictions at the onset. That's where eating low-FODMAP comes in.

FODMAPs

The first goal of treating SIBO is to starve out the bacterial invaders. If they can't eat, they can't reproduce or release inflammatory compounds that damage the digestive tract. So, what do these bacteria eat? You guessed it, FODMAPs. FODMAP stands for Fermentable Oligosaccharides, Disaccharides, Monosaccharides and Polyols. Quite a mouthful! Thank goodness for the acronym. They can also be called fermentable carbohydrates for short.

FODMAPs are the foods to avoid on the SIBO diet. The concept of a low-FODMAP diet was developed by Sue Shepard, Peter Gibson and others at Monash University in Australia to help manage digestive disorders.

In addition to restricting specific foods, a low-FODMAP diet also stresses the importance of eating distinct meals throughout the day and avoiding snacking. This allows time between meals for that migrating motor complex (MMC) to do a thorough sweep of the small intestine. It's also important to slow down at meal time, chew your food completely, and focus on the meal in front of you. Digestion begins in the mouth!

You might be tempted to automatically assume that all FODMAPs are unhealthy foods, since they're on the restricted list, but that isn't the case. In a healthy individual without SIBO, these foods actually contribute to a diverse ecosystem of microbiota in the lower intestine. The main reason we're avoiding them now is because in a patient with SIBO, those same bacteria are living in the wrong place, so we don't want to feed them. Make sense?

The Strict SIBO Diet

It's up to you how aggressively you want to treat SIBO with diet. Dr. Nirala Jacobi, ND, recommends a bi-phasic approach to treating SIBO, which starts out with an extremely restrictive diet and then begins expanding the food list after the first few weeks. Quantities of certain carbohydrate foods change how SIBO-friendly they are as well, so portion control matters on this plan.

The Standard SIBO Diet

Overtime, as your digestive tract heals from SIBO, you can begin to introduce FODMAP foods back into your diet. At the beginning, it's important to be pretty strict about restricting FODMAPs. The standard SIBO diet allows for a greater variety of fruits and veggies, although quantities are still important. Below, we've created a list of high- and low-FODMAP foods in somewhat broad strokes. As you continue to research this way of eating, you might also find that some lists contradict each other. We've done our best to compile the most agreed-upon list of SIBO-specific foods in both categories. Please consult the lists we've linked or the app for more detail.

High-FODMAP foods:
Alliums (garlic, onions, shallots, leeks)

Most brassicas (broccoli, cabbage, cauliflower, kohlrabi — kale is OK)

Asparagus

Legumes (beans and peas; lentils are OK in limited quantities)

Root vegetables (beets, yams, sweet potatoes, potatoes, Jerusalem artichokes, yucca)

Starchy vegetables (artichokes, okra, turnips)

Mushrooms

Certain fruits (In the bi-phasic form of the SIBO diet, initially avoid all fruit except lemons and limes. In a standard low-FODMAP diet, some fruit is allowed. Always avoid jellies, jams and juices.)

All grains

Sugar (includes agave, honey, maple syrup, molasses, sucralose and natural sugar substitutes that end in -ol; stevia is OK)

All conventional dairy products

Bacon sweetened with anything other than honey

All processed lunch meat and deli meat

Condiments that contain sugar or artificial ingredients (catsup, relish, etc.)

Chia seeds and seed flours

Soybean oil

Bouillon cubes or dry seasonings with anti-caking agents or unknown ingredients

Any new eating plan can start to feel pretty restrictive when you focus only on all the foods you can't have. Let's shift to what's allowable on the SIBO diet. In addition to starving out the unwanted bacteria, it's important to begin adding in nourishing foods that are easy to digest and nutrient-dense. Nutrient-absorption is often a problem for SIBO patients, so replenishment is essential.

Low-FODMAP Foods:

• Leafy greens (arugula, lettuce, collards, chard, kale, endive, baby spinach, radicchio, bok choy)

• Certain veggies (bell pepper, bamboo shoots, carrots, eggplant, green beans, cucumber)

• Limited quantities of squash (kabocha, zucchini, yellow squash, butternut)

• Certain fruits (bananas, berries, guava, pineapple, grapes, melon, dragon fruit, kiwi)

• Certain organic dairy products (dry-aged cheese aged at least one month, homemade 24-hour yogurt and sour cream, butter, ghee, dry curd cottage cheese)

• Nuts and seeds (in specific quantities; each nut or seed has its own quantity)

• Organic fats (butter, ghee, coconut oil, olive oil, organic animal fats, MCT oil, polyunsaturated fats except soybean oil)

• Organic unprocessed meats and eggs

• Wild fish

• Bone broth

• Honey (certain sources better than others)

• Stevia (pure, no additives)

Following the SIBO Diet

Reading through this list of foods might feel overwhelming at first, but you'll get the hang of it after a week or so of trial and error. Having a cheat sheet or app with you as a quick reference while you're away from home will definitely help you stay on track and navigate food you're not making for yourself.

Recipes that focus on the low-FODMAP foods, like eggplant and tomato with fresh basil and organic parmesan cheese, or leg of lamb slow-cooked in bone broth with stewed tomatoes and carrots can help you enjoy this process without feeling overly restricted.

Experts don't always agree on which is the best diet for SIBO patients or how long they should stay on such a specific diet. In fact, some conventional GI doctors will simply prescribe an antibiotic (usually Rifaximin) and make no mention of any dietary changes.

Naturopathic doctors like Drs. Siebecker and Nirala stress the use of this therapeutic diet to reduce uncomfortable symptoms and promote the healing process. They argue that to forego the diet is to risk an uncomfortable "die-off" process as the antibiotic or herbal antibiotics do their work of killing off the bacteria. The diet is meant, in part, to make that process more bearable.

Caution: The SIBO Diet Isn't Forever

While we do recommend following the SIBO diet as part of your overall plan to treat SIBO, it's important to remember that this diet isn't meant to last forever. It's a temporary, therapeutic regimen designed to starve out bacteria in the body.

Sharing your body with your microbial inhabitants is critical for healthy immune function, digestive function and fighting chronic inflammation. When the good bugs are in the right place (the colon), we don't want to starve them out.

Once you've removed those bugs from your small intestine, it's important to begin feeding and replenishing the ones in your colon. Slowly reincorporating FODMAP foods and fermented foods, along with possibly supplementing with a good-quality probiotic, will help keep your gut health on track.

Preventing Recurrence

As we mentioned at the beginning, SIBO can be a chronic problem, recurring often and requiring a repeat of the protocol we've outlined here.

The best ways to prevent recurrence are all about making healthy choices, both in the kitchen and in your day-to-day life:

Avoid processed, sugary foods and focus on nutrient-dense foods.

Eat only gluten-free grains or baked goods (sparingly).

Continue eating distinct meals and avoiding ongoing snacking.

Chew each bite of food well before swallowing.

Slow down at meal time and try to focus on eating without the distractions of TV or your phone.

Continue drinking bone broth and consuming probiotic foods.

Find a stress-management practice that works for you.

Every day is a decision about how you will take care of yourself. Choose to prioritize your health and you will be far less likely to relapse.

How Do Antibiotics Treat SIBO and IBS?

First of all, if you don't understand the basics of small intestine bacterial overgrowth which is found in 60-80% of people with IBS, I would recommend reading this article.

Basically, antibiotics treat SIBO by killing the overgrowth of bacteria in the small intestine.

Antibiotics do this by either stopping bacteria from replicating or destroying them. The reason we want to kill bacteria is that people with SIBO have accumulated too many bacteria in their small intestine (there should be much less) which cause debilitating digestive symptoms such as gas, bloating, diarrhea, constipation, fatigue, and abnormal stools.

When you treat this imbalance of bacteria in the small intestine with specific antibiotics, you reduce the amount of gas being produced, which can reduce symptoms.

For some people just treating this bacterial overgrowth can solve the problem, but others will need to address other underlying causes which enabled this bacterial overgrowth in the first place. (We will touch upon prevention later)

Xifaxan for SIBO and IBS

While there are a few different antibiotics usually prescribed to treat SIBO and IBS, the most common antibiotic is Xifaxan (Rifaximin).

Xifaxan is a non-systemically absorbed rifamycin with antimicrobial activity against gram-positive and gram-negative aerobic and anaerobic organisms.

Xifaxan is used to treat traveler's diarrhea, hepatic encephalopathy, IBS/SIBO, and a few other bowel infections.

The main difference between Xifaxan and other SIBO antibiotics is that it is very minimally absorbed throughout the body and works specifically in the gastrointestinal tract.

This means that you are less likely to have toxic or systemic side effects compared to other antibiotics.

Also, the solubility of the drug increases 100-fold in the presence of bile acids (which are delivered directly to the small intestine after eating), meaning that its antimicrobial effect is much greater in the small bowel than in the colon.

More so, Xifaxan decreases mucosal inflammation which is likely another reason it helps IBS patients. Because of these properties, Xifaxan is a top antibiotic chosen for SIBO treatment.

Xifaxan for IBS-D

Xifaxan has been studied and used in all subsets of IBS and SIBO patients including diarrhea, constipation, and mixed type patients. But, it's important to understand that there are differences in the study results when Xifaxan is given under different protocols for diarrhea and constipation type patients. In this section, we will go over Xifaxan's use in IBS and SIBO patients with diarrhea specifically.

Xifaxan is one of the best antibiotics for SIBO and IBS with diarrhea.

In a number of different studies, it has been shown that a 2-week course of Xifaxan at a dose of 550 mg 3 times per day provides significant relief of IBS/SIBO symptoms, such as bloating, abdominal pain, and loose or watery stools.

The only thing you need to keep in mind when using antibiotics is that relapse can occur after treatment, so it's vital to take preventative measures and continue to improve your overall digestive function.

That being said, using Xifaxan for SIBO in patients who have diarrhea as a predominant symptom is usually a very effective option.

Xifaxan Dosages for Diarrhea

• 1200 mg per day for 10 days with 5 g per day of partially hydrolyzed guar gum (source)

• 1650 mg per day for 14 days (source)

Xifaxan for IBS and SIBO with Constipation

Xifaxan is also used in constipation cases but there has been different research findings and outcomes using it with constipation.

It's important to note that usually Xifaxan is used alone only in people with diarrhea or mixed type symptoms, whereas it is used in combination with other medications in constipation-predominant cases.

Despite this, there is some evidence that Xifaxan alone can help some people with constipation, such as this study.

As with all medical treatments, each person has a unique body and using Xifaxan alone for constipation may not be helpful for everyone. But, it has been reported that using Xifaxan in combination with Neomycin (rather then either alone) for constipation can be much more effective.

In this study, patients who tested positive for methane on the SIBO breath test (which usually indicates constipation type symptoms) were split into 3 groups. One group got Xifaxan alone, one just Neomycin, and the last group a combination of Xifaxan and Neomycin.

PROTOCOL DOSAGE METHANE ERADICATION

Rifaximin + Neomycin 1200 mg Rifaximin1000 mg Neomycin

10 days 87%

Neomycin Alone 1000 mg Neomycin10 days 33%

Rifaximin Alone 1200 mg Rifaximin10 days 28%

85% of patients getting combination treatment also noticed an improvement in their symptoms. These results show why Xifaxan alone is not the best option for those with constipation type symptoms; Xifaxan and neomycin work synergistically to treat different organisms in the gut, improving overall symptoms.

Xifaxan Combo Dosages for Constipation

• 1200 mg Rifaximin + 1000 mg Neomycin per day for 10 days (source)

• 1650 mg Rifaximin for 14 days + 1000 mg Neomycin for 10 days

The Pros and Cons of Using Xifaxan for SIBO

There are pros and cons when deciding to use SIBO antibiotics like Xifaxan.

Here is a list of both sides, so you can make the best decision possible

Pros:

• Works quickly when effective

• Protocols have been researched thoroughly

• One of the strongest treatment options

• Xifaxan is a non-absorbable antibiotic so it doesn't cause as many systemic side effects

• Xifaxan can reduce mucosal inflammation

Cons:

• Xifaxan is very expensive, without insurance it usually costs around $1,500

• Xifaxan can still cause negative side effects (though it doesn't happen as often since it acts mostly in the gut)

• You can still relapse after a successful treatment if there is a stubborn underlying cause

• Xifaxan isn't as effective in constipation cases and needs to be combined with Neomycin

Relapse Rates After SIBO Antibiotic Therapy

I think it's important to touch on the relapse rates after using antibiotics for SIBO. This helps you make the decision whether to try natural treatments initially or go straight to antibiotics, especially if you have to do multiple courses.

I think you will find that in the long run, it's important to incorporate a mostly natural strategy, only using pharmaceuticals when your symptoms are very severe.

In this study, the aim was to investigate SIBO recurrence in patients after successful antibiotic treatment. They took 80 patients treated with Xifaxan and reassessed them 3, 6, and 9 months after their breath tests normalized. The results are informative and very important for people who use antibiotics to understand.

The Results:

• 3 months after successful antibiotic treatment 10 patients (10/80 or 12.6%) tested positive for SIBO again indicating relapse

• 6 months after successful antibiotic treatment 22 patients (22/80 or 27.5%) tested positive for SIBO

• 9 months after successful antibiotic treatment 35 patients (35/80 or 43.7%) tested positive for SIBO

They also showed that being older, having your appendix out, and chronically using proton pump inhibitors (like Prilosec) increased the chance of relapse. This means that if you have other health issues that are affecting your gut function you will be more likely to relapse and become a chronic SIBO patient.

This study is very important to understand; it shows that while antibiotics can definitely help a lot, they are only one helpful tool in the overall treatment strategy, and not a magic cure. In reality, many people deal with relapse and have to find a combination of strategies to help maintain their symptom relief while preventing recurrence.

Why Does SIBO Relapse?

This is a great question to ask any doctor or researcher who studies SIBO or IBS. There are many hypotheses right now but no final conclusion. Whoever figures out the solution to the relapse problem will be a rock-star! As mentioned above, SIBO is often a chronic condition, and like the study above showed, recurrence can occur even after a successful course of antibiotics.

It is thought the main reason recurrence occurs is that there is an underlying problem with gut function or the migrating motor complex (MMC).

Some patients who develop bacterial overgrowth have abnormal MMC, meaning that the waves that normally cleanse their small intestine are not effective. Therefore, they do not clear the bacteria and undigested materials as well as other people.

When these small intestine cleansing waves are damaged, it allows bacteria to accumulate, causing SIBO symptoms.

Some of the main prevention strategies which help SIBO patients are:

• Eating a healthy lower carbohydrate diet

• Prokinetic agents (natural or pharmaceutical)

• Fixing other issues that decrease gut motility

• Reducing stress and making healthy life changes (high stress can decrease motility)

What Does it Mean if SIBO Antibiotics Don't Work?

While antibiotics are usually very effective for SIBO (at least in the short term), for others, they may not work at all or for only a very short period of time.

This can be very frustrating. So, what does this mean?

This can mean a few things:

• The SIBO antibiotic protocol was not appropriate for your specific gut bacteria

• You need an additional course of antibiotics or an elemental diet to treat your stubborn microbes

• You have developed antibiotic resistance, meaning the bacteria are not affected by the antibiotics

• You don't really have SIBO, but instead a different type of gut dysbiosis or health issue

• If you relapse very quickly, you may need to focus on figuring out any underlying causes that may be contributing

Can You Treat SIBO Without Antibiotics?

This is an important question many people ask after looking at the SIBO antibiotic relapse rates, side effects, and the cost of purchasing Xifaxan. Yes, you can definitely treat SIBO without antibiotics and in many cases, this may be a better strategy over the long term.

When you realize that most people will relapse after a successful course of antibiotics it makes sense to consider treating SIBO naturally and taking a more gradual approach.

There are a few treatment options that you might find to be effective:

• Herbal antibiotics like Allimed, berberine, oregano oil, and neem

• Elemental diet protocol

• Long-term SIBO diet changes

• Probiotics

Remember that while some treatments work for others, they may not be the best for you. Everyone has a different health history and underlying causes contributing to their issues. It's best to consult with a doctor for specialized advice.

Concluding Thoughts on SIBO Antibiotics

If you're thinking about taking SIBO antibiotics like Xifaxan, know that they can work effectively and quickly. However, a course of Xifaxan is very expensive and you may still have side effects. Also, remember that there is a chance you may relapse once you stop taking the antibiotics.

If you are someone who is dealing with a stubborn case of SIBO- and willing to spend the money on Xifaxan- it can be a good option. On the other hand, if you don't want to spend as much money and want to take a gentler long-term approach, using a natural treatment protocol may be your best bet. Using herbal antibiotics, the elemental diet or long-term diet changes can be just as effective as antibiotics.

What Are Herbal Antibiotics?

First of all, an antibiotic is anything that kills bacteria or other microorganisms. It doesn't matter whether it is made synthetically in a lab or extracted from a plant.

Herbal antimicrobials are simply natural antibiotics that are extracted from herbs grown around the world or in your own garden. Humans have been relying on plant medicines—and particularly antibiotics for thousands of years.

Plants—just like humans have evolved defense mechanisms, such as their own antibiotic substances, to protect themselves from bacteria, viruses, fungi and other parasites. Humans developed a complex immune system—but plants, powered by the sun, developed a pretty astonishing array of substances that these plants use to defend themselves against infection.

Differences Between Herbal and Prescribed Antibiotics

Herbal antibiotics for sibo vs regular

The main difference between antibiotic herbs and prescribed antibiotics is the source and the purification methods used.

Prescribed antibiotics are synthesized in a lab and consist of only the antibiotic and various fillers needed to make the capsule, tablet or liquid form of the antibiotic. These antibiotics usually have a single mechanism of action (MOA) that attacks one aspect of the life cycle or the structure of the microorganism. Some antibiotics damage the cell wall of bacteria, causing death by leakage. Others damage the microorganism's ability to reproduce. In addition, they only work on one type of microorganism. Anti-bacterial medicines, for example, do not affect viruses or fungi.

On the other hand, antimicrobial preparations from herbs are made from whole plants and contain many different compounds. These plant medicine combinations usually have a range of MOA's and extracts from one plant can often have anti-bacterial, anti-fungal and anti-viral effects. Herbal antimicrobials can be given as tinctures (usually in alcohol), as teas, in capsules or tablets or as lotions or salves to apply directly onto the skin.

The mixture of plant substances that are extracted have some distinct differences—and often advantages—as compared to a purified, synthetic antibiotic. These differences include:

A mixture of substances—with a variety of MOAs—decreases the risk that antibiotic-resistant bacteria will arise

In general, the anti-bacterial and anti-microbial compounds derived from plant sources tend to spare the healthy gut bacteria a little more, decreasing the risk of diarrhea and other complications of antibiotic therapy.

While plant sources of antibiotics tend to be less specific than prescribed, synthetic antibiotics, the overall risk of adverse effects also tends to decrease with herbs

Components in herbs are believed to act synergistically – in other words, the sum of the effects of the plant substances is greater than when using a single plant substance.

The Rise of Antibiotic-Resistant Strains of Bacteria

Since the introduction of synthetic antibiotics, bacteria have been able to adapt quickly to these purified compounds. It makes quite a bit of sense, after all. The "life purpose" of bacteria is to reproduce, grow and colonize—since the bacteria can double in number very quickly, they have lots of chances to try out new ways to escape the selective pressure put on them by synthetic antibiotics.

So, in order to survive, bacteria evolve new ways to evade the effects of antibiotics—they become antibiotic resistant.

Herbal formulas give them fewer opportunities for this—partly because plants have been making antibiotics for a lot longer than humans have, and partly because the mixture of substances provide a diversity of MOAs and spare the healthy bacteria which can quickly grow to "reclaim" the territory that the infectious pathogenic bacteria were colonizing.

Why Antibiotic Herbs Work for Treating SIBO

intestines

SIBO stands for small intestine bacterial overgrowth. This is a condition in the gut that occurs when too much bacteria build up in the small intestines. When this occurs the bacteria can feed on carbohydrates and produce many uncomfortable symptoms such as nausea, bloating, gas, diarrhea, constipation, and more.

SIBO is usually caused by slow movement of the intestines, structural issues with the bowel, malabsorptive disorders, immune system dysfunction, or medications like narcotics that slow down motility. You can learn more about SIBO with our guide here.

While the only way to cure SIBO is to fix the underlying cause leading to bacterial overgrowth (such as impaired GI motility), antimicrobials are currently one of the most effective treatment options used by practitioners to reduce bacterial overgrowth in the small bowel helping to resolve symptoms.

Treatments used for SIBO are typically one or a combination of the following:

Antibiotics

Herbal Antimicrobials

Elemental Diet

Probiotics

Dietary changes

Prokinetic agents

This means that both herbs which have antibiotic effects and conventional antibiotics are used by practitioners to treat SIBO while also working on fixing any underlying causes.

Herbal vs Regular Antibiotics for SIBO

So, you're dealing with SIBO and you're deciding whether to take a regular antibiotic like Rifaximin (Xifaxan) or try a SIBO natural therapy protocol using herbs.

In certain situations, either protocol can be a good option. Let's compare the difference between using herbal formulas and pharmaceutical drugs.

PHARMACEUTICALS VS HERBS FOR SIBO PRESCRIBED ANTIBIOTICS HERBAL ANTIMICROBIALS

Effectiveness Varies: Depends on the antibiotic, the dose and how long prescribed Varies: Depends on the combination of herbs, the dose, and how long used. A recent study showed that herbal treatment was as effective as Rifaximin for SIBO.

Cost $100's to $1,000's $10's to $100's

Side Effects Potential for more severe side effects Relatively mild side effects

How Long Before See Improvement May see improvement 1-2 weeks after beginning Usually takes 3-4 weeks to see improvement if not longer

Accessibility Prescription needed No prescription needed

Both herbs and pharmaceutical drugs have their benefits. Keep in mind:

Pharmaceutical antibiotics usually work quicker but cost more and you will need a prescription from your doctor. They also have the potential for more harmful side effects since they are stronger.

On the other hand, herbal antimicrobials can be just as effective but often take up to 4-5 weeks to work effectively. You can get herbs online and a prescription is not required.

But, it's important that if you do decide to take any form of antibiotic, including natural formulas, to take them correctly because they can still cause side effects.

Who Should Use Herbal Antibiotics for SIBO?

who should use herbal antibiotics?

You should consider using herbal antimicrobials for SIBO if:

If you have financial difficulty purchasing a prescription for Xifaxan or don't want to spend $100s to $1,000s on drugs that aren't covered by insurance.

If you have used regular, prescription antibiotics in the past and want to find a cheaper and less harsh way of treating SIBO.

If you don't have easy access to a doctor.

If you are someone that has a more holistic mindset, natural medicine can be a great option.

The Best Natural Antibiotics for Treating SIBO

herbs

There are a number of different herbs with antibiotic properties. In fact, there have even been a few studies like this one that concluded "herbal combinations prove just as effective as standard prescription antibiotics", making them a good substitute option for conventional prescriptions.

Also, keep in mind that different herbal combinations are usually chosen based on the gases produced in your gut and the symptoms you are experiencing. For example, for sibo methane gas treatment herbs that work on methane producing organisms like Allimed and Atrantil are usually chosen.

Below are a few of the different herbs that can be used to treat SIBO. The dosage used is usually 1-3 of the herbs taken 2-3x a day for 6-12 weeks.

Allimed

Oregano Oil

Berberine

Neem

Pomegranite Husk

Clove

Thyme

Atrantil

Below are 2 other combination formulas that have been proven effective in a study. The dosage used was 2 caps twice a day for each product in the combination formulas.

Dysbiocide + FC Cidal from Biotics Research or

Candibactin AR + Candibactin BR

Experiences with SIBO Herbal Treatment Protocol

Many people have tried a few different SIBO treatments of which one or two have been helpful. Herbal antimicrobial formulations in the form of capsules and tinctures can be very helpful to balance gut flora, but you have to weigh that in the face of how effective they may be—or how long it may take to feel better.

Combining these natural antimicrobials with a soothing herbal tea can be super helpful for many. The synergistic effect when using teas along with tinctures or capsules can be very powerful—and can help increase effectiveness and the speed with which you may respond.

One of the capsule protocols people report success with includes:

Allimed (2 capsules 3x per day for 4 weeks)

allimed herbal antibiotic

Berberine complex (2 capsules 3x per day for 4 weeks)

berberine complex

Using Other Preparations of Herbs

herbal tea and antibiotics

Other herbal preparation methods besides using capsules can also be effective. Many people have had success using tinctures and high strength herb teas. These can be made at home by soaking herbs in alcohol or purchasing them from companies which make the tinctures or teas.

Even if you plan to take the capsules it might be beneficial to incorporate herb teas into your health protocol because the immune boosting and synergistic effects of combining different herbs can make your capsule protocol more potent.

For example, fresh ginger root tea or licorice root tea may increase the effectiveness of the capsules. If you want to learn more about making tinctures or teas there are plenty of herbalism education books you can purchase.

Ginger Root Tea (Recipe from Herbal Antibiotics):

Juice a few pieces of fresh ginger (3-4 pieces the size of your thumb)

Combine ¼ cup of ginger juice with 12 ounces of hot water, ⅛ teaspoon of cayenne, ¼ lime juice, 1 tablespoon of wildflower honey (if you can tolerate it)

Drink 4-6 cups throughout the day during your treatment protocol

Licorice Root Tea:

Add 1 tablespoon of licorice root to 1 liter of simmering water in a kettle. Simmer on low for 20 minutes

After 20 minutes add 2 tablespoons of the following mix: passion flower, chamomile, lemon balm (mixed in equal amounts), then take off the heat and let the mixture steep for 15 more minutes

Strain the final liquid product into a large container and drink throughout the day

Herbal Therapy for SIBO FAQ's

How Do I know if I Have SIBO?

In order to tell if you have SIBO, the test that is most often used by doctors is a hydrogen and methane breath test. This test measures the amount of hydrogen and methane gas produced in the small intestine when feeding the bacteria a sugar solution of lactulose. See our guide to breath testing here.

Is SIBO Serious?

Yes, SIBO is serious because it can dramatically impact someones quality of life and cause numerous frustrating digestive symptoms. Although, it has been shown that SIBO is not a fatal condition.

Can SIBO Be Cured Permanently?

Yes, SIBO can be cured permanently if the underlying cause is fixed. Some of the most common underlying causes are impaired intestinal motility, medications like narcotics, immune system disorders, and anything else that inhibits normal gut motility.

What is the Strongest Antibiotic for Bacterial Infection?

The strongest antibiotics for bacterial infections are herbs like oregano oil, clove, thyme, berberine, and conventional antibiotics like Xifaxan and Neomycin. It's always best to use them carefully to avoid microbiome disruption because they often times have a more broad spectrum effect on bacterial populations.

What to Avoid While on Antibiotics?

While on antimicrobials it's best to avoid very restrictive diets, excessive alcohol use, and any other lifestyle habit or medication that can interfere with treatment efficacy.

What Happens if You Take Probiotics and Antibiotics at the Same Time?

If you take probiotics and antibiotics at the same time some studies have shown that you may be able to reduce your risk of pathogenic infection and microbiome disruption. A lot of practitioners recommend using probiotics alongside antibiotics but there are some who do not. The evidence is not entirely clear on this issue and there needs to be more research conducted.

How Do You Restore Good Bacteria After Antibiotics?

The best way to restore good bacteria after using antibiotics is to focus on healthy diet and lifestyle habits including adequate sleep, whole plant foods, exercise, and positive social activity. Some people might also benefit from including fermented foods such as kombucha and sauerkraut as well as probiotics while others with SIBO may not be able to tolerate these foods.

What to Keep In Mind with SIBO Natural Treatment

Remember, when you are going through any SIBO natural treatment, you need to work on resolving any underlying causes.

There is a reason this bacteria is accumulating and potentially recurring following treatments.

It may be because of a weakened immune system, poor gut motility, adhesions, or from another drug you are taking. It can also be due to your dietary habits—at least for a few weeks, try switching to a whole food organic diet emphasizing vegetables, fruit, and fish.

Also, consider trying some high-potency (and high quality) strain specific probiotics—or try eating yogurt with active cultures. Other fermented (and non-pasteurized) foods can provide probiotics as well. Fermented foods include kefir, kombucha, sauerkraut, pickles, miso, tempeh, natto and kimchi. Some people may see benefit from adding in a therapeutic strain probiotic. Others may need to wait.

You can also try including a specific prebiotic in your diet as well to see if it helps—partially hydrolyzed guar gum has shown some success in IBS studies.

It's important that you work to strengthen your whole body so that you can prevent SIBO recurrence. The goal is to get your gut working more like a smooth flowing river, not a spastic backlogged one.

This may mean transitioning to a healthy diet, improving immune function so you can fight off invaders, getting adequate sleep, or improving your hormones and gut motility—or ALL of those things. Yes, using antibiotics for SIBO can be a very necessary part of your healing journey but keep in mind that if you don't improve your overall health the antimicrobial protocols may not have the same effect.

The Mediterranean Action Plan

The Mediterranean Action Plan can greatly reduce your risk of heart disease and

stroke. An anti-inflammatory Mediterranean diet is full of vegetables, fruits,

beans, nuts, seeds, fish, chicken, and healthy fats, such as those from extra-virgin

olive oil.

Those following an anti-inflammatory Mediterranean diet may want to avoid

or limit nightshade vegetables, soy products, and red wine or alcohol.

RULES AND PRINCIPLES

Consume plenty of fruits and vegetables. Most fruits and vegetables are

welcome staples on this diet. Be aware, though, that some recipes

corresponding to this diet contain nightshade vegetables like tomatoes, peppers, and eggplant. Try them and see how you feel afterward. If you have

a reaction, eliminate nightshades for two weeks and see if there is

improvement.

Limit gluten-free grains. While a limited amount of grain is allowed in a

typical Mediterranean diet, an anti-inflammatory dieter may want to reduce

grain consumption further.

Eat healthy sources of fat. Oily fish, such as wild salmon, sardines,

anchovies, and trout, are wonderful sources of omega-3s, making them a

perfect fit for this plan. Aim to eat fish two to three times per week.

Skip the red wine. Many are drawn to a traditional Mediterranean diet

because it allows one or two glasses of red wine per day. However, it's best to

omit the wine, and avoid alcohol altogether, as it can aggravate inflammatory

conditions.

POTENTIAL BENEFITS

A reduced risk of heart attack or stroke.

Animal products are allowed.

POSSIBLE CHALLENGES

If you enjoy that glass of wine with dinner, you might feel disappointed or deprived.

If you have trouble with nightshades, particularly tomatoes, you may not react

as well to this diet.

The Paleo Action Plan

Paleo followers consume red meat, wild game, poultry, eggs, nuts, seeds, fish,

vegetables, and fruits. However, since we know that excess consumption of

animal products can lead to inflammation (particularly if it comes from feedlots),

this anti-inflammatory plan includes less meat.

RULES AND PRINCIPLES

Consume fewer animal products, particularly red meat. Traditional Paleo

plans include large quantities of meat, including beef, lamb, chicken, eggs,

and fish. This anti-inflammatory menu reduces the consumption of red meat and chooses more fish and poultry. Instead of eating animal products at

virtually every meal, try to consume more vegetarian meals.

Buy organic, pasture-raised animal products. Animals raised on hormones,

antibiotics, and GMO grains can increase inflammation levels; additionally,

the meat from these animals contains higher amounts of omega-6 fatty acids.

Organic, pasture-raised meat is richer in anti-inflammatory omega-3 fats.

Eat plenty of fruits and vegetables. Most vegetables and fruits are allowed on

this meal plan. That said, it is recommended that you eliminate nightshade

vegetables (potatoes, tomatoes, peppers, eggplant, etc.).

Be mindful of egg consumption. The traditional Paleo plan includes plenty of

eggs. However, if you are intolerant, eliminate them.

Include gluten-free pseudograins. Quinoa, amaranth, and buckwheat are

often referred to as grains because of the way they are cooked and used, but

they are actually not grains at all—they are seeds. They are gluten-free and rich in nutrients, such as amino acids. Consuming these pseudograins can be

beneficial to anti-inflammatory Paleo followers who are trying to eat less

meat.

POTENTIAL BENEFITS

Increased consumption of plant-based foods, most of which are naturally antiinflammatory.

Improvement in symptoms if dealing with an inflammatory condition and,

perhaps, even eliminating or reducing medication.

POSSIBLE CHALLENGES

Consuming a lot of organic, grass-fed animal products, along with nuts and

seeds, can be expensive.

Difficulty finding high-quality sources of animal products.

A grain-free and nightshade-free diet can feel restrictive and limited.

Common Risk Factors for SIBO

Common Risk Factors for SIBOResearchers suspect SIBO is caused by a combination of decreased pancreatic enzymes, bile acids and gut motility.

Consequently, certain health conditions or lifestyle choices may increase your risk of developing SIBO:

Gastrointestinal infections: Such as post-infectious IBS (Irritable Bowel Syndrome)

Chronic use of antacids: Long-term antacid use (such as omeprazole) reduces acid production in the stomach. Consistently low levels of stomach acid can lead to bacterial overgrowth in the stomach and small intestine.

Immunodeficiency Syndrome: Disorders that can suppress our immune system – such as AIDS and IgA antibody deficiency – provide an ideal environment for harmful bacteria to thrive .

Celiac disease: Celiac disease can disturb how food moves through the intestines, particularly if it remains undiagnosed or is poorly managed. This leads to increased bacterial growth in the gut.

Aging: In general, older people are at increased risk for SIBO because our digestive tract gets weaker with age. This is thought to be caused by reduced physical activity, weight gain, ongoing medication use and general weakening of the gastrointestinal tract.

Alcoholism: Chronic alcohol consumption appears to increase risk of SIBO.

Gastroparesis: There is a strong overlap between symptoms, and it seems those with gastroparesis (also known as delayed gastric emptying) are more likely to have SIBO.

Numerous other conditions are linked with increased SIBO risk, but more research is needed. These include hypothyroidism, Crohn's disease, ulcerative colitis, fibromyalgia, rheumatoid arthritis, Parkinson's disease and more.

Your risk of SIBO is greatly increased by several conditions and factors, most often related to reduced function and efficiency of the intestines.

SIBO Symptoms

SIBO symptomsMany SIBO patients experience different signs and symptoms.

These often overlap with other conditions such as IBS. The most common problems are:

Fatigue

Nausea and vomiting

Bloating and diarrhea

Poor nutrient absorption leading to deficiencies

Malnutrition and weight loss.

Some people may also experience depression and skin problems like acne and eczema.

The intensity of symptoms can differ, too.

While some patients may have diarrhea and milder vitamin deficiencies, others may experience severe nutrient malabsorption and impaired digestion.

Nutrient Deficiencies

Left unmanaged for several months, SIBO can cause several vitamin and mineral deficiencies.

Vitamin B12 deficiency is one of the most common deficiencies, alongside the fat-soluble vitamins such as A, D, E and K .

Mineral deficiencies such as iron, calcium and magnesium are also common in SIBO patients.

SIBO symptoms range from digestive stress to severe nutrient deficiencies. They are often similar to IBS.

Diagnosing SIBO: Hydrogen Breath TestSIBO is a severely under-diagnosed condition .

This is because a large portion of our small intestines is impossible to reach without surgery.

Fortunately, some non-invasive tests have been designed; namely the Hydrogen Breath test. This same test can be used to detect common food intolerances, IBS and H. pylori infection.

Breath Test for SIBO

The two types of Hydrogen Breath Test used for SIBO are the Lactulose Breath Test (LBT) and the Glucose Breath Test (GBT).

Both tests measure concentrations of hydrogen and methane in the breath.

While neither is perfect, the LBT seems to be preferred.

SIBO-breath-test

How a SIBO breath test works.

These two gases are only produced by bacteria (in the small intestine) and not directly by humans. High levels indicate increased bacterial activity and/or overgrowth.

In order to give an accurate reading, prior to the test patients follow a specialized diet for 1-2 days that does not feed the bacteria. On the day of the test, a formulated sugar drink is given in order to get a clear reading of the patient's reaction to carbohydrates.

The test can be done with take-home kits or with your doctor in the clinic. But interpretation of results should always be with a health care professional.

 The best non-invasive method for diagnosing SIBO is with a Hydrogen Breath Test. Request with your doctor if they have been unable to pinpoint your digestive symptoms.

First Line of Treatment: SIBO and Antibiotics

sibo and antibioticsDiet alone will not rid of SIBO, so you'll need antibiotics or herbs (or both) as your first line of treatment.

Conventional treatment for unwanted bacterial growth is antibiotics.

Antibiotics are designed to kill bacteria, which is why they are prescribed when you have an infection.

The usual antibiotics used are rifaximin, ciprofloxacin or metronidazole.

Rifaximin is the most well-studied antibiotic for SIBO, with a success rate of about 50% after 1 week. A combination of rifaximin and other antibiotic, neomycin, has been shown to be around 85% effective after 10 days.

Here is the recommended therapy, according to information from a SIBO symposium in 2014:

Patients with a positive hydrogen breath test: 550 mg rifaximin 3 times per day for 14 days (not missing any doses).

Patients with a positive methane breath test: 550 mg rifaximin 3 times per day + 500 mg neomycin twice a day for 14 days. Alternatively, 550 mg rifaximin 3 times per day with 250 mg metronidazole 3 times per day for 14 days.

Foods allowed:

Meat, chicken, fish, eggs, some legumes, lactose-free dairy, ripe fruit, non-starchy vegetables, nuts and seeds, and honey.

Foods not allowed:

All grains, starchy vegetables (such as potato, corn), regular dairy, some legumes, sugar.

Basically it shares many similarities to the low FODMAP diet, but not as much scientific backing at this stage. More studies are underway and I'm looking forward to the results.

GAPS Diet

The Gut and Psychology Syndrome diet (GAPS diet) is similar to SCD but with a few modifications.

It contains a different introductory phase, fewer legumes, and dairy protein is reintroduced more slowly.

There is some anecdotal evidence to support it, but these are for autism and other conditions related to brain function (hence the name) rather than digestive issues.

There are no studies of the GAPS diet in the medical literature, and the creator makes a lot of extraordinary claims, which is often a red flag.

The SCD and GAPS diet have emerged as potential diets to help treat SIBO, but neither was actually designed for this condition. They may be useful, but are not evidence-based.

Unproven Treatments

SIBO sufferers have looked to other alternative treatments to help reduce their symptoms and rid of bacterial overgrowth.

Keep in mind that these are all anecdotal, and there has been little to no research on these potential treatments. Be sure to check with your doctor before trying any option mentioned below.

Iodine

Some have claimed that taking iodine — namely Lugol's 5% iodine — has helped them rid of SIBO.

However, the role of iodine as an effective antibiotic for the gut has yet to be studied.

It's important to remember that iodine directly affects your thyroid. Discuss with your doctor before starting any protocol, especially if you experience thyroid issues.

Peppermint and Other Essential Oils

Enteric-coated peppermint oil has proven to be effective in reducing symptoms like bloating in patients with IBS .

In this study, the researchers found that peppermint oil decreases the production of hydrogen, a bacterial byproduct in patients with SIBO.

Other essential oils — including oregano, tarragon, frankincense, wormwood, and clove oil — may also lend some relief.

Do know that these oils can be potent. Before starting any essential oil regimen, check with a skilled practitioner to help you determine exact dosing.

Intermittent Fasting

Some people believe that intermittent fasting can help "starve" the bad bacteria.

But this may not rid of the bacteria completely. Instead, starving them may make them harder to eradicate.

Under-researched

SIBO remains largely overlooked and under-researched.

According to the education and research nonprofit International Foundation for Gastrointestinal Disorders, less than 1% of digestive disease research funding is provided for functional disorders, including SIBO.

This results in many doctors and patients not realizing how common SIBO is. Plus, many SIBO symptoms overlap with those of other digestive disorders. This makes it even more difficult to distinguish SIBO from IBS or lactose intolerance.

The good news is that there are effective SIBO treatments that can restore gut health.

This guide breaks down the basics of this complicated condition so you can better understand how the proper diagnosis, medical care, and dietary changes will help rid you of the symptoms of this frustrating condition.

Causes

A healthy gut is essential for a strong immune system. When gut bacteria become imbalanced, it puts a person's overall health in jeopardy. Causes of this imbalance can stem from:

Poor eating habits (processed foods and added sugars)

Stress

Illness

Extended use of antibiotics

As well as other contributing factors

Combine any of these causes, and you may experience any number of digestive disorders, including SIBO.

Prohibited Foods on the SCD:

Sugar, molasses, maple syrup, sucrose, and processed fructose including high-fructose corn syrup or any processed sugar

All grain including corn, wheat, wheat germ, barley, oats, rice, and others. This includes bread, pasta, and baked goods made with grain-based flour

Canned vegetables with added ingredients

Some legumes

Seaweed and seaweed byproducts.

Starchy tubers such as potatoes, sweet potatoes, and turnips

Canned and most processed meats

Canola oil and commercial mayonnaise (because of the additives)

All milk and milk products high in lactose such as mild cheddar, commercial yogurt, cream, sour cream, and ice cream.

Candy, chocolate, and products that contain FOS (fructooligosaccharides)

Allowed Foods on the SCD:

Meats without additives, poultry, fish shellfish, and eggs

Certain legumes, including dried navy beans, lentils, peas, split peas, un-roasted cashews and peanuts in a shell, all-natural peanut butter, and lima beans

Dairy limited to cheeses such as cheddar, Colby, Swiss, dry curd cottage cheese, and homemade yogurt fermented for at least 24 hours

Most fresh, frozen, raw or cooked vegetables and string beans

Fresh, raw or cooked, frozen or dried fruits with no added sugar

Most nuts and nut flours

Most oils, teas, coffee, mustard, cider or white vinegar and juices with no additives or sugars

Honey as a sweetener

While more scientific research is needed, some clinical studies published in the Journal of the Academy of Nutrition and Dietetics show that the SCD diet is effective for reducing IBD symptoms and achieving remission

GAPS Diet

An acronym for Gut and Psychology Syndrome, the GAPS diet was created as a modification to the SCD diet. It has a focus on the connection between the gut and the brain.

The theory is that many conditions affecting the brain are caused by a leaky gut, which allows chemicals and bad bacteria from your food to enter the bloodstream when they normally wouldn't.

However, this is a highly controversial theory and more research is needed to prove or disprove its legitimacy.

There are two parts to the GAPS diet: The Introduction Diet and the Full GAPS Diet.

People with severe digestive issues and severe food sensitivities are recommended to start with the Introduction Diet. Details of the Introduction Diet for GAPS can be found here.

Those suffering from constipation and mild symptoms should start with the Full GAPS Diet. Details about the Full GAPS Diet can be found here.

Fast Tract Diet

The Fast Tract Diet was developed by Norm Robillard, Ph.D. It uses a points-based system to help people manage their symptoms by tracking their intake of fermentable carbohydrates, which have been scored according to fermentation potential.

It is similar to the low FODMAP diet, but also includes some additional foods that may cause symptoms. It is often successful for people who failed a low FODMAP diet.

Antibiotics

Just as an overgrowth of bacteria can lead to compromised gut health, so too can a deficiency of good bacteria.

Given that antibiotics destroy good bacteria along with harmful bacteria, antibiotic treatment is not an ideal long-term solution.

On the other hand, closely monitored antibiotic treatment can help, since diet alone will not cure SIBO.

Targeting not just the bacterial overgrowth — but the types of bacteria colonizing the small intestine — is essential. Fortunately, prescription antibiotics given by a medical doctor can be a viable option.

Studies show the success rate of herbal antibiotics as equivalent to the results of using pharmaceutical antibiotics.

Probiotic Supplements

Taking probiotic supplements is another strategic tool for treating SIBO. One study showed that adding a lactol probiotic helped maintain bacterial overgrowth in the small intestines.

Specific strains of probiotics may help to promote motility, reduce intestinal permeability and reduce methane gas. Although the idea of using probiotics for SIBO seems counterintuitive, they are part of a successful treatment strategy when carefully selected.

But it's important to take the right probiotic strains based on your specific symptoms. Probiotics, for example, may exacerbate your issues, if an incorrect strain is used.

If you decide supplements are right for you, we recommend these high-quality products:

Culturelle

Healthy Origins Natural Healthy Fiber

Florastor Daily Probiotic

Path to Gut Health

If you're suffering from SIBO, it can be a difficult road getting your body back on track, especially when SIBO is so often misdiagnosed and often under-diagnosed.

The good news is that it's manageable. While the solution to SIBO is likely not found in one approach, knowing the different options can provide a holistic view of how to treat this condition effectively.

And, as always, you can get gut updates and stunning nature imagery from our popular Facebook page. Also, scroll down for our best gut articles.

THE CAUSES OF SIBO

In healthy people, the small intestine is kept relatively clean. Food is received in the stomach where it is mixed with acid and other digestive juices, which transforms your food into a clean substance. This slurry gets pushed through the small intestine where the body absorbs nutrients. The waste gets dumped into your large intestine where it absorbs water making the feces more solid before they are expelled from the body in a bowel movement.

Our gut is full of bacteria, much of which is good for us, this intestinal flora is vital to the efficient healthy workings of the digestive system. Intestinal flora helps us to digest important vitamins such as vitamin K and folic acid while also protecting the intestine against invasion by harmful bacteria, the type of bacteria that causes disease.

However, if normal intestinal functions are compromised then an overgrowth of bacteria can occur. There are several reasons why this could happen; it may be caused by insufficient stomach acid or result from intestinal damage from alcohol or toxins for example. It could also be caused by the small intestine transferring waste material to the large intestine (or colon) less efficiently.

RISK FACTORS

As I mentioned in the introduction, SIBO is often linked to underlying illnesses which affect the way in which the small intestine functions. Bacterial growth is generally kept in check through a number of bodily protective mechanisms such as intestinal mobility i.e. the way in which it moves contents through the digestive system, and also stomach acidity. Our body's bile content also hinders bacterial growth while our ileocecal valve prevents stools from refluxing out of the colon into the small intestine.

An illness or a disease of some kind which harms the body's defensive mechanism can put a person at a greater risk of SIBO. However, it is most often a motility problem of the intestines that lead to a person developing SIBO. Examples of this include complications following a gastric bypass operation, tumors and bowel strictures or adhesions.

Certain neurological diseases such as Parkinson's disease and myotonic dystrophy may also affect bowel motility as can diabetic neuropathy.

Other diseases linked to an increased risk of SIBO are:

Celiac disease

Crohn's disease

Diverticulitis

Alcohol abuse and liver cirrhosis

Achlorhydia (a chronic inflammatory condition which prevents the stomach from producing acid)

Leukemia

Lymphoma

Scleroderma

SYMPTOMS AND DIAGNOSIS

A SIBO diagnosis is difficult because there are no actual specific symptoms that can lead to a direct diagnosis. Instead, SIBO is considered as one of a variety of unspecific symptoms which put together can lead to a diagnosis.

INITIAL SYMPTOMS

The initial symptoms affecting the digestive system and stomach include one or more of the following:

Abdominal pain

Diarrhea

Indigestion

Bloating and flatulence

LONGER TERM SYMPTOMS

As the condition continues to progress, the overgrowth of bacteria prevents the body from being able to effectively absorb the nutrients from food. This can lead to a range of problems such as protein deficiencies, vitamin deficiencies, electrolyte imbalance and problems with absorbing fat.

The body's inability to properly absorb vitamin B 12 can lead to a variety of symptoms associated with anemia including peripheral neuropathy and decreased red blood cell numbers. A reduced level of vitamin A can cause night blindness while a deficiency in vitamin D can cause metabolic diseases that lead to spasms and bodily twitches.

The malnutrition symptomatic of SIBO is likely to result in dramatic weight loss and muscle wasting. The body's difficulty in absorbing fats from the diet can cause a condition called steatorrhea, a condition characterized by an excess of fat in you feces which in turn leads to oily and foul smelling stools and possible anal leaking.

SO, COULD YOUR DIET BE CAUSING SIBO?

The bacteria that inhabit our gut is not always harmful. There are a host of friendly bacterial strains often referred to as intestinal flora which perform a number of important bodily functions. These roles include a range of functions from aiding the digestive process to regulating your mood. And like any other living organism, bacterium needs to nourish itself and feed off something in order to survive. And the stuff they primarily like to feed off is carbohydrates

The standard modern western diet tends to be full of carbohydrates and not just any carbs, but typically simple carbohydrates like starchy and sugary foods. Your intestinal flora will dine out on these excess carbohydrates causing them to thrive, proliferate and causing you to have an overgrowth issue.

Another problem with the standard western diet id that it is rich in inflammatory food such as gluten which can damage the stomach's lining and reduce the level of stomach acid necessary to regulate bacteria.

As I mentioned earlier, there are 5 generally accepted diets for SIBO which all aim to starve the bacteria and prevent it from overgrowing in the small intestine.

1. THE LOW FODMAP DIET

This is a very popular and effective diet for SIBO which was originally designed to treat irritable bowel syndrome but can easily be adapted for the purposes of SIBO.

The diet is based on getting rid of the food that contributes towards fermentation in the intestines.

Because it was designed for IBD and is also an excellent choice for IBD, the low FODMAP plan does not eliminate either polysaccharide or disaccharide carbohydrate sources such as starch, grain or sucrose. In most people these types of carbohydrates are easily absorbed but in the case of SIBO they should also be eliminated from your diet as bacteria enjoy feeding off them.

A comprehensive list on food allowed and not allowed on a low FODMAP diet can be found here, but remember it will need to be adapted for SIBO.

THE SCD DIET

The SCD diet was originally created to treat Celiac disease before being popularized in a book written by Elaine Gottschall. SCD is an acronym for Specific Carbohydrate Diet and like the FODMAPS diet; it is designed to starve bacteria to prevent them from taking hold.

The SCD diet restricts complex carbohydrates, sucrose, lactose and other man made products. These types of carbohydrate are considered to be generally unhealthy and even somebody without SIBO would do well to follow it to a certain extent.

Carbs of this kind encourage bacteria to feed and can lead to bacterial as well as yeast overgrowth and other inflammatory conditions.

The SCD is a very popular and effective diet with excellent success rates. Estimates from surveys suggest the success rate is over 75% from following this diet.

EXAMPLES OF FOOD NOT ALLOWED ON THE SCD DIET INCLUDE:

• Grains and cereal

• Canned vegetables

• Canned fruit

• Processed meat products

• Potatoes

- Dairy products

- Fava beans

HOWEVER, DO NOT DESPAIR, THERE ARE PLENTY OF ALLOWED FOODS THAT ALLOW YOU TO HAVE AN INTERESTING AND VARIED DIET INCLUDING:

- Fresh meat products

- Spices

- Kale and lettuce

- Mushrooms and peppers

THE CEDAR-SINAI DIET PLAN FOR SIBO

Unlike the 4 diets we have already spoken about which are designed to treat SIBO and other inflammatory conditions of the intestines, this diet is actually designed for those of you concerned about getting it in the first place.

This preventive diet which was designed by Dr. Pimentel is not as strict as the ones already discussed but it does follow similar principles. The essential idea is that you reduce your intake of food which your body finds difficult to digest thus ensuring that harmful bacteria do not use them to feed off.

As well as the dietary requirement, the doctor who devised the plan in the first place recommends that you eat infrequently because of the way in which this can affect the migration of food through the intestines which in turn affects bowel movement and cleanliness.

FOOD TO AVOID ON THIS DIET INCLUDES:

- Dairy products

- Artificial sweeteners

- Legumes such as beans and lentils should be limited

- Soda

- Beer

- Tea and coffee should also be drunk only in moderation

YOU SHOULD HOWEVER:

- Drink at least 8 cups of water each day

- Eat proteins such as fish, beef and eggs but in moderate amounts

- Eat moderate quantities of fruit

- You can eat vegetables but only if they are the non-starchy variety

SO WHICH DIET SHOULD I CHOOSE?

I don't blame you for being a bit confused at this point. There are so many similarities and minor variations between the diets that it is difficult to know which one to opt for. Couple with the fact that many of these diets were originally designed with another condition in mind; it makes it an even more difficult choice.

Fortunately there is a specific SIBO diet plan that takes its lead from the diets listed above but tailors it towards the SIBO disease far more specifically.

This specifically designed diet is basically a combination of the SCD diet and the low FODMAP's diet that we have already discussed above. It is considered to be an especially effective diet for those with stubborn cases of the disease and when alternative diets have not proven successful.

Unlike the other recommended diets which were designed to treat similar conditions, this diet was created to treat SIBO in particular by Dr. Siebeckar who is a renowned SIBO expert.

Like the other diets, the aim is to starve and kill the bacteria which cause the overgrowth and the basic tenets of the diet are similar to the others that we have talked about.

THIS DIET REQUIRES YOU TO FOLLOW THESE RULES:

• Starch must be avoided

• Low fiber

• You should eat only small amount of fermentable fruit and vegetables

• Avoid raw food and beans to begin with

• Be careful about the size of your portions

• Wait 4 hours at least between meals

The things that you can eat allow for a varied and enjoyable eating experience...

YOU CAN EAT AS MUCH AS YOU WISH OF CERTAIN FOODS INCLUDING:

• All types of meat

• Dairy products as long as they are free of lactose

- Fat

HOWEVER CERTAIN TYPES OF FOOD ARE RESTRICTED AND BASED ON A TIER SYSTEM INCLUDING:

- Fruit

- Vegetables

- Nuts and seeds

WHAT YOU CANNOT EAT ON THE SIBO SPECIFIC PLAN:

- Grains including oats and quinoa

- Sugar

- Thickeners like gum and agar

- Corn and soy

- Beans (at the beginning of the regime)

- Mucilaginous food such as seaweed, astralagus, licorice and slippery elm

- Garlic and onions

There are 60 to 70 million Americans suffering from some sort of digestive disease, with nearly 50 million visiting the doctor each year. (1) Unfortunately, the Standard American Diet (SAD) combined with the hectic lifestyles many of us lead are likely contributors to these staggering statistics.

We rush through our meals, eat processed foods and give ourselves little time to recover from the hustle and bustle of each day. This lifestyle is taking a toll as we forego nutrient-dense foods that take time to prepare in favor of foods that actively do damage to our gastrointestinal tract overtime. Irritable Bowel Syndrome (IBS) affects 15.3 million Americans, while Ulcerative Colitis and Crohn's disease add almost another 1 million to the mix. (1)

SIBO isn't listed in the U.S. Digestive Disease Statistics, but it could be contributing to these three ailments or could be a result of them, along with a number of other digestive disorders. SIBO stands for Small Intestinal Bacterial Overgrowth. This complex syndrome is often responsible for chronic cases of diarrhea or constipation. SIBO sometimes causes IBS or is mistaken for it. (2)

The solution isn't simple, but with proper testing, medical care, diet and lifestyle changes, SIBO is curable and controllable. We're going to break down everything you need to know about SIBO, including the special diet that goes along with it.

CONCLUSION

Dietary changes for SIBO can be an important part of your treatment protocol to reduce symptoms, but it's important to understand that diet is just one of the treatment strategies alongside antibiotics, prokinetics, and fixing underyling causes. It's necessary that you still meet all of your nutritional requirements and do not cause nutritional deficiencies by restricting too many foods.

In summary, the Low FODMAP or low fermentation diet has shown the best research results for helping people with SIBO, so trying this dietary approach can be helpful to identify the combination of carbohydrates your body tolerates best. `

A healthy and diverse gut bacteria is important for health.

Made in United States
Troutdale, OR
05/08/2024

19741486R00037